3 0132 02490277 2

Northumberland Schools Library Service	
3 0132 02490277 2	
Askews & Holts	Apr-2017
S914.93 ORANGE	£12.99

D1639737

BELGIUM

WORLD ADVENTURES

BY STEFFI CAVELL-CLARKE

BookLife

©2017
Book Life
King's Lynn
Norfolk PE30 4LS

ISBN: 978-1-78637-138-6

All rights reserved
Printed in Malaysia

Written by:
Steffi Cavell-Clarke

Edited by:
Charlie Ogden

Designed by:
Danielle Jones

A catalogue record for this book
is available from the British Library.

BELGIUM
WORLD ADVENTURES

CONTENTS

Page 4   Where is Belgium?

Page 6   Weather and Landscape

Page 8   Clothing

Page 10   Religion

Page 12   Food

Page 14   At School

Page 16   At Home

Page 18   Families

Page 20   Sport

Page 22   Fun Facts

Page 24   Glossary
                  and Index

Words in **red** can be found in the glossary on page 24.

WHERE IS BELGIUM?

Belgium is a small country in the western part of Europe. Belgium lies between France and Germany.

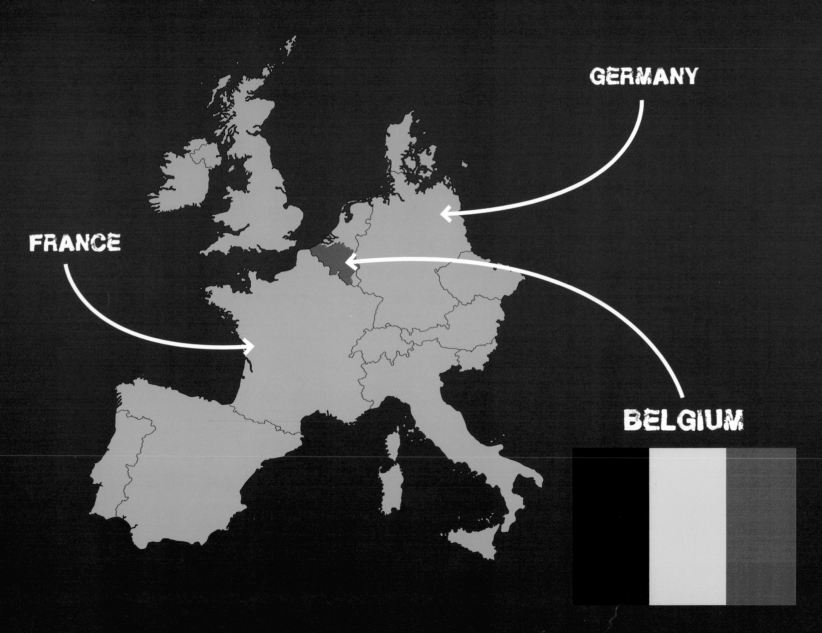

GERMANY

FRANCE

BELGIUM

The **population** of Belgium is over 11 million. Most people in Belgium live in large towns and cities.

The capital city of Belgium is Brussels.

BRUSSELS, BELGIUM

WEATHER AND LANDSCAPE

The weather in Belgium changes with the seasons. It is often hot and sunny in the summer and cold in the winter.

There are many different types of landscape in Belgium. There are long rivers, meadows, fields and woodlands.

CLOTHING

Most people in Belgium wear **modern** clothing. Some men and women wear smart clothing when they go to work.

The costumes worn at the Carnival of Binche.

Traditional clothing is sometimes worn in Belgium. During the Carnival of Binche, men and women often wear traditional **costumes** and masks.

RELIGION

The **religion** with the most followers in Belgium is Christianity. Most of the Christians in Belgium are **Roman Catholic**.

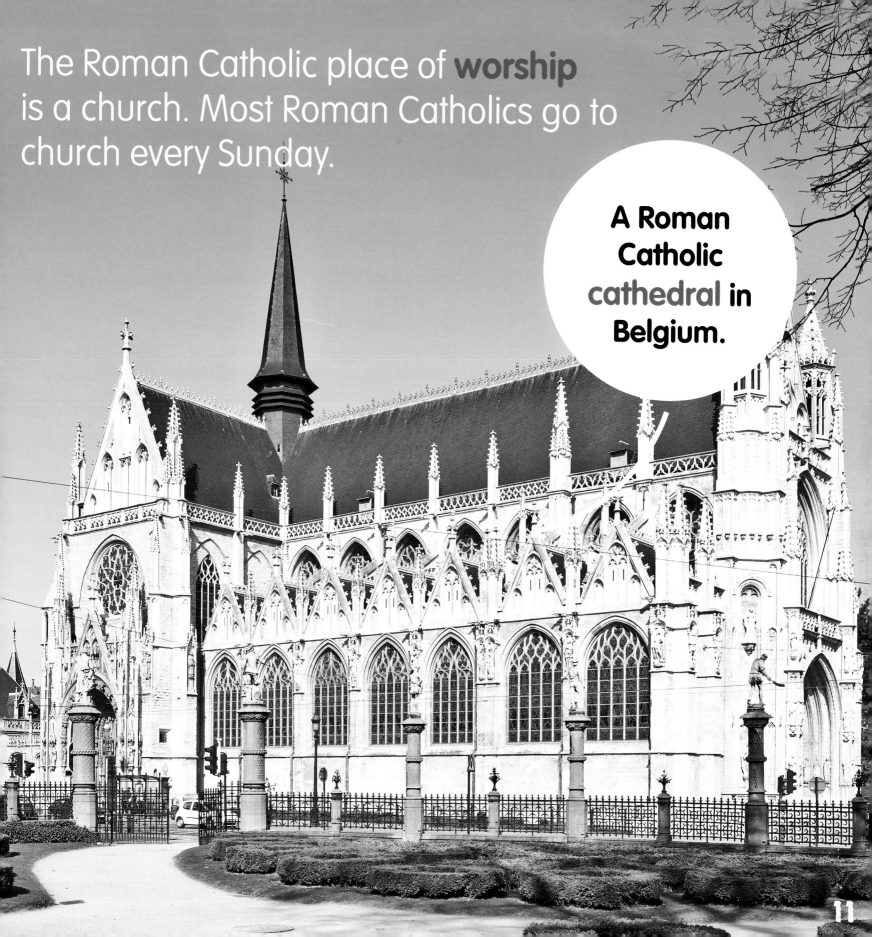

The Roman Catholic place of **worship** is a church. Most Roman Catholics go to church every Sunday.

A Roman Catholic **cathedral** in Belgium.

FOOD

Belgium is famous for its chocolate. Belgian chocolate can come in all different shapes and sizes. It is often eaten as a treat or given to a loved one as a gift.

Beer is a popular drink for adults in Belgium.
There are lots of different Belgian beers and they
are enjoyed by people all over the world.

AT SCHOOL

Children in Belgium have to study until they are 18 years old. Not all children go to school. Instead, some children are taught at home.

Many children in Belgium go to after-school clubs where they can play games and sports. Lots of children like to play football.

AT HOME

APARTMENTS IN BELGIUM

Many people in Belgium live in large towns or cities. They usually live in houses or apartments.

There are also people who live in villages or on farms. Farmers in Belgium often grow lots of fruit and vegetables.

FAMILIES

Most children in Belgium live with their parents and **siblings**. Some children also live with other family members, like their grandparents.

Lots of Belgian families like to get together for special occasions, such as weddings and birthdays.

SPORT

Football is one of the most popular sports in Belgium. Lots of people follow Belgium's **national** football team.

Belgian fans showing their support for their football team.

Many people in Belgium also like cycling. Lots of people visit Belgium to cycle through the beautiful landscapes.

FUN FACTS

People in Belgium celebrate many festivals throughout the year. They often celebrate by playing music and wearing costumes.

ROYAL PALACE
OF LAEKEN

Belgium has its own royal family. They live in a large building in Brussels called the Royal Palace of Laeken.

GLOSSARY

cathedral	a large building used for Christian worship
costumes	clothes that make a person look like someone else
modern	something from present or recent times
national	relating to a specific country
population	the number of people living in a place
religion	the belief in and worship of a god or gods
Roman Catholic	a member of the Roman Catholic Church
siblings	brothers and sisters
traditional	ways of behaving that have been done for a long time
worship	a religious act such as praying

INDEX

chocolates 12

Christianity 10

clothing 8–9

farms 17

festivals 22

football 15, 20

homes 14, 16–17

landscapes 6–7, 21

royal family 23

schools 14–15

seasons 6

towns 5, 16

Photocredits: Abbreviations: l-left, r-right, b-bottom, t-top, c-centre, m-middle.
Front Cover l – Andresr. Front Cover r – Aleksey Klints. 2 – Botond Horvath. 5 – S-F. 6 – Sergey Novikov .7t – Regien Paasen 7m – Kotomiti Okuma. 8 – bokan. 9 – skyfish. 10 – wavebreakmedial. 11 – pbombaert. 12 – Jiri Hera. 13 – Click Images. 14 – Africa Studio. 15 – Rawpixel.com. 16 – Christian Mueller. 17 – Dan Thornberg. 18 – g-stockstudio. 19 – IVASHstudio. 20 – katatonia82. 21 – defotoberg. 22 – Anibal Trejo. 23 – Philip Lange. Images are courtesy of Shutterstock.com, unless stated otherwise. With thanks to Getty Images, Thinkstock Photo and iStockphoto.